RUBBISH AND RECYCLING

ROSIE HARLOW AND SALLY MORGAN

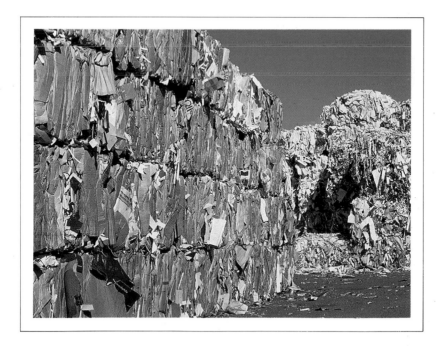

KING*f*ISHER

KINGFISHER
Kingfisher Publications Plc
New Penderel House
283–288 High Holborn
London WC1V 7HZ

First published by Kingfisher
Publications Plc 1995
This edition published 1999
10 9 8 7 6 5 4 3 2 1
1TR/0499/WKT/UNV(HBM)/128KMA

Copyright © Kingfisher Publications Plc 1995

A CIP catalogue record for this book is
available from the British Library.

ISBN 1 85697 382 4

Printed in Hong Kong / China

About This Book

This book looks at the problems of producing too much rubbish and explains how recycling it can help to make our environment a cleaner and safer place. It suggests lots of experiments and things to look out for, as well as ways to reduce, reuse and recycle our waste.

You should be able to find nearly everything you need for the experiments in and around your home. Be sure to wear rubber gloves whenever you are handling rubbish or litter.

Activity Hints

- Before you begin an experiment, read through the instructions carefully and collect all the things you need.
- When you have finished, clear everything away, especially sharp scissors, and wash your hands.
- Start a special notebook so you can keep a record of what you do in each experiment and the things you find out.

Contents

What a Waste!

People produce loads of rubbish. Throughout the world, we create a billion tonnes of it each year. Even cavemen produced it. Their caves soon filled with old bones, wood and other waste, so eventually they had to move to a new cave. Today we throw away more rubbish than ever before. But many of the things we think of as, rubbish are not waste at all. They are made from valuable materials taken from the environment (called raw materials) that *could* be used again.

Wasted Cars

In the USA, over seven milllion cars are scrapped each year. The metals can be recycled, but that still leaves a lot of waste, including millions of tyres.

restaurant waste

litter

garage waste

household waste

Instead of being thrown away, much of the rubbish seen here could be reused, or recycled, to make new things. This would mean taking fewer raw materials from our environment.

Do it yourself

Do a packaging survey.

Much of the rubbish we throw out comes from packaging – the materials used to wrap food and other goods we buy from shops. Next time you or a member of your family go shopping, count the number of layers of wrapping on some of the items. Packaging holds the goods together and makes them look attractive. But often you will find there are lots of unnecessary layers.

chocolate wrappers

lid

tray

protective layer

paper

base

a box of chocolates may have up to six layers of packaging

cakes may have up to four layers

lid

cellophane

cake

base

tray

box

tray

toys usually have few layers

toy

office waste

industrial waste

shop waste

today

20 years ago

These are just some of the many things we think of as waste. But the real waste is throwing away so many valuable materials such as paper, glass, wood and metals. Even kitchen waste can be reused.

Getting Lighter

In the last 20 years, the packaging used for supermarket goods has become one-third lighter. This helps to cut down on waste and saves energy.

Where Does It Go?

Each week, our rubbish is put out in dustbins to be collected and taken away. Much of it ends up being buried in a landfill. This is a big hole in the ground, such as a disused quarry or sand pit. But burying rubbish takes up a lot of space and spoils the countryside. Sometimes the rubbish is taken to an incinerator where it is burned. The heat may be used to make electricity for local homes. But burning it produces harmful fumes that pollute the air.

Energy from Waste

Burning rubbish to make electricity is a useful way of getting rid of waste. One dustbinful of rubbish can generate as much electricity as a bag of coal.

Not all rubbish is wasted. Rotting rubbish gives off a gas called methane which can be burned to make electricity. Kitchen and garden waste can be made into compost and sprayed on fields. And many materials can be recycled.

burned in an incinerator

methane gas used to make electricity

buried in landfill

used as compost

recycled to make new goods

Rubbish put in a landfill is squashed down before more rubbish is placed on top. Eventually, the hole is filled completely. Then it may be covered with soil and turned into a park or sports ground.

Recycling is a good way to help our planet. It saves materials, energy, and land that might otherwise be used as landfill. It also reduces pollution.

Do it yourself

Do a charity clear-out.

Charities collect a wide range of items that might otherwise get thrown away. Find out what your local charity shop collects and have a charity clear-out at home. Instead of being burned, your waste could end up helping someone.

foreign coins

Christmas cards

old books

old knitting needles

used telephone cards

drinks cans

old records and tapes

used stamps

7

Nature's Recycling

Have you noticed that you never see huge piles of dead trees and animals in woodlands? This is because natural materials quickly decompose (break down) and are recycled. These materials are said to be biodegradable. Nature is very good at recycling, so nothing goes to waste. Minibeasts, earthworms, fungi and microscopic bacteria are important because their job is to break down the wastes. They are called decomposers.

 Eye-Spy

Look out for waste that is biodegradable. Apple cores, dead leaves, old clothes, cardboard boxes and newspapers will all eventually rot or get eaten.

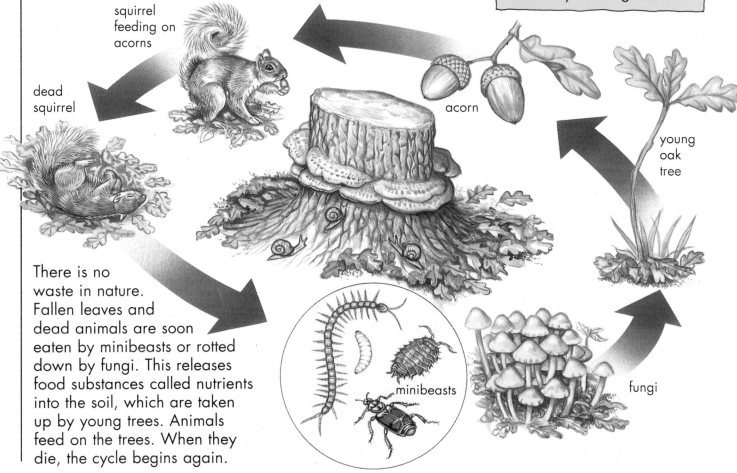

squirrel feeding on acorns

dead squirrel

acorn

young oak tree

There is no waste in nature. Fallen leaves and dead animals are soon eaten by minibeasts or rotted down by fungi. This releases food substances called nutrients into the soil, which are taken up by young trees. Animals feed on the trees. When they die, the cycle begins again.

minibeasts

fungi

Do it yourself

Catch some minibeast decomposers using this simple method.

1. Cut a piece of thick paper about 30cm x 20cm. Roll it up to make a funnel shape and tape it together. The hole at the bottom should be about 1cm across.

folding paper into cone

glass jar

black paper   tissue

thick paper   tape

2. Put some damp tissue in the bottom of a glass jar and wrap the jar with a piece of black paper. Put your funnel in the jar.

3. Collect some leaf litter from under some trees. (Leaf litter is a damp mixture of rotten leaves and soil.)

Worms at Work

Worms are good recyclers. They feed on dead and rotting matter, such as leaves, that they find on the ground. This helps to break the matter down so it can be reused by plants.

4. Fill your funnel with leaf litter and leave the jar sitting under a strong light from a table lamp for two hours. Minibeasts prefer dark damp places, so the ones in your leaf litter will try to crawl away from the heat and light of the lamp. They will soon fall through the bottom of the funnel into the jar.

More Things To Try

Build a home for your decomposers by turning a large jar on its side. Make breathing holes in the lid and put some soil, rotten wood and leaf litter inside, along with your minibeasts. Add plenty of food such as apple or potato peel and keep the soil damp. Then cover the jar with a dark cloth. Return the creatures to their natural habitat after a few days.

minibeast decomposers

decomposers' home

Rubbish That Won't Rot

If you left a plastic bag, a glass bottle, or an aluminium can outside, it would stay there, unchanged, for hundreds of years. This is because plastic, glass and metal are non-biodegradable – they will never rot. Of course, it is important for some materials to be non-biodegradable. Buildings materials, glass and many plastics must stay intact to do their job properly. But when they are no longer needed, these materials are difficult to get rid off.

nuts   nails

Much of the rubbish we throw out each week will never rot. We have to keep creating new landfill sites to take it all. One day, our planet could become one big rubbish tip!

cling film

plastic bottle

polystyrene box

drinks can

Do it yourself

Do a litter survey to find out how much litter there is in your street, around your school and in your local park.

Draw a chart like the one shown below. Mark on your chart how much litter you find in each place and what kind of litter it is. Clear the litter up as you go by putting it in a bin liner. Be sure to wear gloves when you touch litter.

	STREET	PARK	GARDEN
GLASS	LHT	IIII	II
PAPER	LHT	IIII	LHT
PLASTIC	II		

How Can We Help?

- Never drop litter – rubbish that is made of plastics, polystyrene, metals and glass will not rot away.
- Do a litter survey like the one here, and organize a 'litter blitz' to clear it all up.

crisp
packet

glass

👁 Eye-Spy

Because most litter does not rot, it will stay in our environment for many years unless it is cleared up. Check the dates on litter, such as crisp packets, to see how old it is.

cooking foil

batteries

Litter gets everywhere, from our streets to our beaches, and it is not a pretty sight. People who drop non-biodegradable waste outdoors are spoiling the environment for everyone else.

Do it yourself

Find out which rubbish is biodegradable and which is not by doing this simple test.

1. Collect some yoghurt pots or plastic cups and fill them with damp soil.

2. Find several bits of man-made rubbish and several bits of natural rubbish. Bury each object in a pot and identify it with a label. Leave the pots somewhere cool and damp for a couple of weeks, then dig up the objects to see if they have rotted or changed at all.

How It Works

The natural rubbish will have started to decompose or may have rotted away altogether because it is biodegradable. The man-made rubbish does not decompose and will not have changed at all. Luckily, we can recycle much of our non-biodegradable rubbish so that it can be used again.

yoghurt
pots

soil

banana skin

paper

leaf

marble

nail

lid

sweet wrapper

potato peel

11

Waste Not, Want Not

It is very wasteful to throw things away if they can be reused or recycled. Raw materials have to be taken from the environment to make new things, which uses energy and causes pollution. So, the more we throw away, the more the environment will be harmed. The number of materials we can recycle is increasing all the time. Once, only glass and metal were recyclable. Nowadays, we can also recycle paper, cardboard, rags, batteries, plastics and much more.

👁 Eye-Spy

Next time you empty a bottle or drinks can, finish a comic or tear a T-shirt, think about whether the leftovers can be recycled.

Christmas Recycling

Instead of throwing out your old Christmas tree with the rubbish, take it to a recycling centre where you may be able to get it chipped into tiny pieces for reuse as garden compost.

- **30%** waste paper and cardboard
- **30%** kitchen waste
- **10%** metal
- **10%** glass
- **8%** plastics
- **4%** old clothes
- **8%** other materials, including dust

This diagram shows the different amounts of waste that get thrown out in our rubbish each week. If we were more careful, we could recycle three-quarters of our household waste.

Do it yourself

Find out how much rubbish your family produces in a week and sort it into bags ready for recycling.

1. Find seven plastic carrier bags and tape a piece of scrap paper on to each one so you can write down what it contains. You will need a bag for each of the following: metal, paper, cardboard, plastics and polystyrene, glass, old clothes and fabrics, and food scraps.

2. Sort your rubbish into the different bags and see how much you collect in a week. How does your rubbish compare with the amounts shown in the diagram opposite?

sorting rubbish into different bags

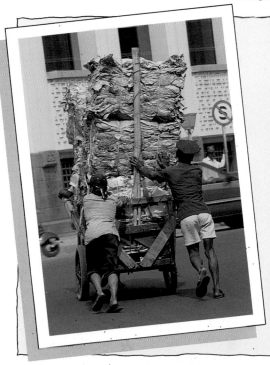

Nothing Wasted

The people in many poorer countries are far better at recycling than we are. They cannot afford to throw away things like plastic bags and bottles, which we take for granted. All their rubbish is carefully sorted so that any useful materials can be recycled. This couple is collecting cardboard boxes for recycling in Jakarta, in Indonesia.

How Can We Help?

We should all try to cut down on the amount of rubbish we produce. The best way to do so is to remember the three Rs – that is, *reduce, reuse* and *recycle*.

We can reduce waste by buying less in the first place, reuse items such as carrier bags and glass jars instead of throwing them away, and recycle our rubbish so that materials are not wasted.

Gardens and Garages

A lot of recycling can be done at home. For example, biodegradable kitchen and garden waste, such as food scraps and grass cuttings, can be put on a compost heap. The waste quickly rots down to form a compost which makes a good fertilizer (food) for garden plants. Your garage may be full of old junk that usually ends up on the local rubbish dump. Some of it might find a new life as a flower container or a water butt.

Fallen leaves can be recycled by digging them into the soil. As they rot, the leaves form a substance called humus which makes a good plant food.

Do it yourself

Build a compost heap or 'worm factory' for your kitchen waste so you can recycle food scraps into a rich compost that will help your plants to grow.

1. Ask an adult to drill two lines of holes around the bottom of an old dustbin as shown on the opposite page. This will allow any liquid to drain out of your bin.

2. Put a layer of gravel or stones, about 18cm deep, in the bottom of your bin. Follow this with a layer of sand about 8cm deep. The sand and stones will allow water to drain through your bin while still keeping the contents damp.

sand

gravel

kitchen waste

cocoshells

brandling worms

slats of wood

How Can We Help?

- Never pour waste oil down the drain – it causes water pollution.
- Put garden waste on a compost heap or take it to a recycling centre.
- Use old pieces of wood to make bird tables or nesting boxes.

wheelbarrow

oil drum

car battery

old tools

used oil

old tyre

broken spade

chimney pot

old tyres

recycled plant pots

Old tyres and chimney pots, and broken wheelbarrows, can be recycled to make unusual flower containers. Plant pots are often made of recycled materials.

Some garages take old tyres, oil and car batteries for recycling. Or you can take them to a recycling centre, along with any broken tools.

3. Add a layer of wooden slats to stop the compost mixing with the sand. Put about 15cm of cocoshells (potting compost) on top.

4. Buy some brandling worms from a fishing shop and lay them in the coco-shells. Feed them regularly with kitchen waste, such as fruit and vegetable peelings, cabbage leaves, crushed eggshells and cheese rinds. Do not feed them meat or fruit.

5. Leave the lid on your worm factory to keep it warm and damp. The compost will be ready to use on your garden after two to three months.

6. Pick out the worms before you put the compost on your garden. Return them to their worm factory so they can get back to work!

kitchen waste

worms in cocoshells

wooden slats

sand

gravel

15

Down the Plug Hole

Every day, we each use litres of water cleaning ourselves and flushing the toilet. We also use water for cooking, and in dishwashers and washing machines, as well as for washing the car. Once we have finished with the water, it disappears down the drain. But that is not the last we see of it. It is then cleaned and recycled so we can use it again. There always seems to be plenty of fresh water. But sometimes, if there has been a drought, there is hardly enough to go round. So we must all try to reduce the amount of water we use.

How Many Times?

In many large cities, water from the tap has been recycled as many as 20 times! But it is still perfectly safe to drink.

Do it yourself

Do a water survey to see how much water is used at home by your family in a day.

Draw a chart like the one here, listing all the things that use up water in your home, such as boiling a kettle, flushing the toilet or having a bath. Mark it on your chart each time someone uses water. How is water used most often? Could you think of ways to use less water?

	How often
Kettle	⊥⊥⊥⊥ I
Cooking	II
Washing up	I
Washing Machine	II
Dish Washer	I
Toilet	⊥⊥⊥ II
Bath	II
Watering plants	I
Hose pipe	

your home

The Water Cycle

treatment plant

rain falls

reservoir supplies homes with water

water evaporates

clean water pumped into river

Dirty water from your home goes to a treatment plant to be cleaned. Then it is poured into rivers and carried to the sea. Some water evaporates (turns into a gas) and forms clouds. When rainwater falls, it fills up the reservoirs that supply us with water.

Do it yourself

See how quickly water evaporates.

Measure out 50ml of water into each of three different containers – a saucer, a glass and a bottle. Leave them on a sunny windowsill for a day.

From which container has most water disappeared?

How It Works

The water evaporates fastest from the saucer because it has a large surface area open to the air. It takes longest to evaporate from the bottle because there is little surface area open to the air and only a small hole to escape through.

17

Do it yourself

Water is cleaned at a treatment plant by filtering it through soil, sand and gravel to remove all the dirt. Try making your own water filter.

1. Line a funnel with a coffee filter paper or blotting paper. Put a layer of fine sand, about 4cm deep, in the bottom of the lining paper.

2. Mix a handful of soil with some water. Pour the dirty water into the funnel and see how well the sand filters out the soil. Does the water come out clean?

glass jar

sand

soil

funnel

coffee filter paper

water

How It Works

As the water trickles through the sand, pieces of dirt are trapped by the sand particles and the water is cleaned.

How Can We Help?

Save water – it is too precious to waste.
- Turn taps off so they don't drip.
- Take a shower instead of a bath – you will save 30–50 litres every time.
- Put a brick in the cistern so less water is wasted when you flush the toilet.

Water containing sewage (human waste) is treated at a sewage farm (shown left). The solids are removed, then the liquid part is trickled through filter beds where bacteria break down any germs.

Plenty of Paper

Paper is a very useful material. It is used to make books, newspapers, bank notes, writing paper, kitchen paper and much more. Most of it is made from conifer trees. The wood is chipped into tiny pieces and mixed with water and chemicals to produce a pulp. Then it is drained, squeezed and dried to form a huge roll of paper. Paper and card are easily recycled. The old paper is chopped up and put back into the paper-making process at the pulping stage.

Eye-Spy

This symbol is used to show that something has been made from recycled paper. How many things can you spot in your house that have this symbol on?

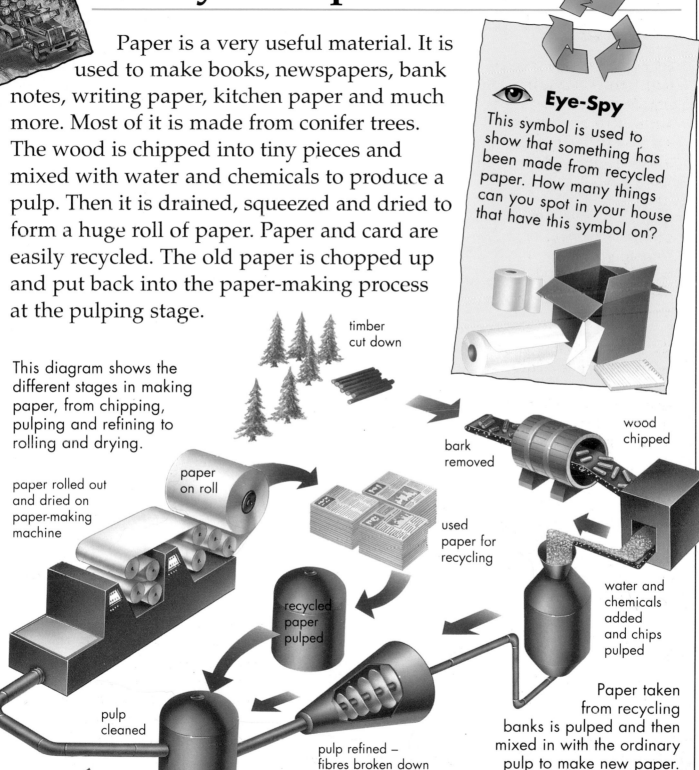

This diagram shows the different stages in making paper, from chipping, pulping and refining to rolling and drying.

timber cut down

paper rolled out and dried on paper-making machine

paper on roll

bark removed

wood chipped

used paper for recycling

water and chemicals added and chips pulped

recycled paper pulped

pulp cleaned

pulp refined – fibres broken down

Paper taken from recycling banks is pulped and then mixed in with the ordinary pulp to make new paper.

Why Recycle It?

Recycling paper means less rubbish needs to be buried in landfills. Making new paper from old also saves on chemicals, energy and water. But it does not really save trees because most paper is made from conifers that are grown specially for this purpose.

Paper and cardboard is tightly packed into bales, ready to be recycled. If we did not recycle our paper, we would need to cut down five million trees every day!

How Can We Help?

- Take newspapers and cardboard to your local recycling centre.
- Reuse old envelopes by putting a sticky label over the old address.
- Whenever possible, draw or write on both sides of your paper so you don't waste any.
- Collect scrap paper and staple it together to make a phone messages pad.

The trees used for making paper come from conifer plantations. As trees are cut down, new trees are planted in their place, so there is a constant supply of wood. Unfortunately, the plantations replace natural habitats such as peat bogs and heathlands that are rich in wildlife. By recycling paper we are helping to save wildlife.

How Much Paper?

On average, a person in the USA uses 310kg of paper every year, almost twice as much as someone in the UK and 100 times more than in India.

USA 310kg

UK 165kg

India 3.2kg

Do it yourself

Make some recycled paper. You will need an adult to help you.

1. Tear up several newspapers into thin strips and leave them to soak in a bucket of water overnight.

washing-up bowl

saucepan

newspaper

nails

plastic mesh

wooden frame

hammer

tacks

2. Ask an adult to boil the mixture in an old pan for 10 minutes until the paper dissolves into a mushy stew. Leave it to cool. Then pour the mixture into a wide flat washing-up bowl.

3. Now ask the adult to help you make a frame that will fit into your bowl. You will need to cut four lengths of wood and nail them together at the corners.

4. Cut a piece of fine plastic mesh slightly bigger than your frame. (You can buy the mesh from a garden centre. Choose a mesh with holes less than 5mm across.) Tack or staple the mesh on to the frame.

scooping the frame under the pulp

paper pulp

5. Starting with the frame held upright, scoop it into the bucket and under the pulp that is floating on the surface of the water. Then lift the frame out flat so that there is an even layer of pulp all over it.

6. When the water has drained away, turn the pulp out on to a piece of felt or an old blanket. Add two more layers of pulp.

7. Place another piece of felt or blanket on top, then a hard board. Tread on the board to squeeze out all the water, then remove the top blanket and board and leave the paper to dry.

hard board

felt

paper pulp

felt

Banks for Bottles

Glass has been used for thousands of years. It is made by heating sand, soda and limestone together at very high temperatures so that they melt and form a liquid. As the liquid cools, it turns into glass. Glass is easy to recycle. The old glass is cleaned and broken up, then it is melted and moulded into shape just like new glass. Recycling means taking fewer raw materials from the ground. It also helps to save energy.

Buying milk and orange juice in returnable glass bottles saves energy and raw materials because the bottles can be reused up to 11 times. A carton can only be used once.

crushing glass

hot glass

glass for recycling

melting glass in furnace

bottle mould

bottle bank

supermarket

filling and capping bottles

Glass from a bottle bank is cleaned and broken up into small pieces called cullet. The cullet is melted down in a furnace and the liquid glass is then poured into a mould and left to cool. The bottles are filled and capped, ready for our supermarket shelves.

A mountain of glass lies waiting to be recycled. Glass is sorted into different colours before it is processed. Clear glass is the most useful because it can be made into all kinds of bottles and jars, but green glass has fewer uses – it is mostly made into wine bottles.

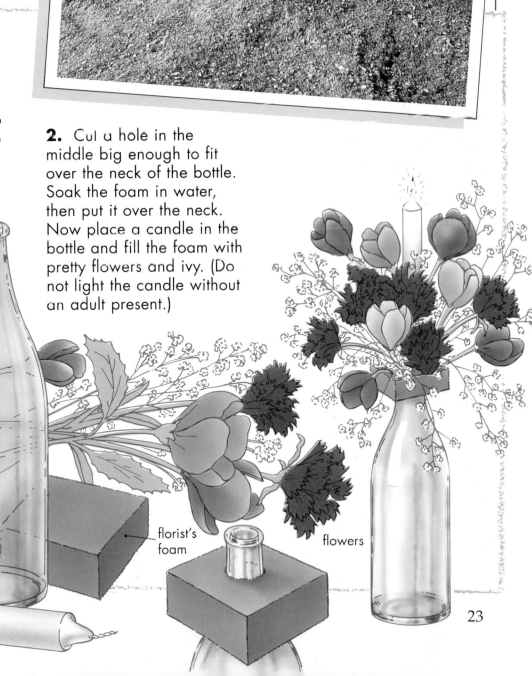

Do it yourself

Instead of recycling it, reuse a glass bottle to make this pretty table decoration.

1. Buy a block of florists' foam from a flower shop and cut off a small piece about 8cm square and 4cm deep.

2. Cut a hole in the middle big enough to fit over the neck of the bottle. Soak the foam in water, then put it over the neck. Now place a candle in the bottle and fill the foam with pretty flowers and ivy. (Do not light the candle without an adult present.)

glass bottle

florist's foam

flowers

candle

23

How Can We Help?

- Take unwanted glass to a bottle bank to be recycled.
- Buy milk, orange juice and yoghurt in reusable glass bottles rather than cartons and pots whenever possible.
- Reuse bottles and jars as containers or vases (see below for ideas).

bathroom tiles

reflective road signs

Not all recycled glass is used to make new bottles and jars. Some is used to make bathroom tiles, bricks, reflective road signs, and fibreglass boats and canoes.

bricks

fibreglass boat

Do it yourself

Make a bottle orchestra.

Collect some empty bottles and jars of all shapes and sizes and wash them out. Fill them with different amounts of water to give a range of notes, then 'play' them by tapping them with a metal spoon. See if you can play any tunes you know.

playing bottle with metal spoon

More Things To Try

Reuse glass bottles and jars by turning them into containers for pens and pencils, flowers, marbles and much more. Paint them with jazzy designs or glue paper scraps or stamps all over them.

Cans Count

Metal food cans have been used for about 200 years. Cans are ideal for storing food and drink for long periods. We use millions of them every day. The metal used in cans is valuable, so recycling is very important. There is no limit to the number of times the metal can be recycled. Steel made from old cans uses just one quarter of the energy that would be needed to make steel from raw materials. Recycling also means digging up fewer raw materials, creating less rubbish and filling up fewer landfills.

What to Recycle?

All sorts of metal items can be recycled, including steel and aluminium food and drinks cans, bottle tops and aluminium foil and frozen food trays.

Cans in Space

Every year, more than 16 billion cans are used in the UK alone. If they could be lined up end to end, they would stretch to the Moon and back twice!

Everything made of steel contains some steel that has been recycled. The steel in a can of beans could end up in a bridge, a car, a knife, or just a simple paper clip.

cutlery

scissors

kitchen knives

refrigerators

bridges

paper clips

cars

Aluminium and Steel Cans

The first cans were made from iron coated with a thin layer of tin, which is why we still call them tin cans. Nowadays cans are made from steel or aluminium. Drinks cans have to be light, so they are made from a very thin sheet of metal. Food cans have to be thicker and stronger so they can protect their contents.

Inside a recycling plant special machines are used to squash aluminium cans into bales. The cans are then melted down and rolled out to form sheet aluminium, ready to be used again.

👁 Eye-Spy

Most drinks cans now have a symbol, or logo, on their side, reminding you to recycle them. Here are some of the logos to look out for.

Do it yourself

Do this simple test to see if a can is made of steel or aluminium.

Steel is magnetic – that is, it is attracted to magnets – and aluminium is not. So hold the can up to a magnet and see if it sticks. If it does, it is made of steel. If it does not, it is made of aluminium.

Check other metal objects to see if they are magnetic, such as needles, keys, pencil sharpeners, knives, foil and bottle tops. If they are, they are made of steel or iron.

magnet

can

Saving Energy

The amount of energy needed to make one aluminium can from raw materials is the same as that required to make 20 cans from recycled aluminium.

How Can We Help?

- Take your food and drinks cans to your local recycling centre.
- Encourage your school to get a can bank so you can all collect cans for recycling.
- Don't forget that foil, bottle tops, and take-away metal trays can be recycled too!

Do it yourself

Use a couple of empty food cans and a length of string to make your own 'mobile phone'.

food cans

nail

hammer

knotting string

string

1. Ask an adult to file down any sharp edges on the cans. Then wash them out.

2. With an adult's help, make a hole in each can, in the centre of the base, using a hammer and nail.

3. Cut a piece of string 20 metres long. Feed each end through a hole in the base of the cans. Tie the ends off with a knot on the inside.

4. Ask a friend to hold a can up to his or her ear and stand as far away from you as possible. Keeping the string pulled tight, speak into your can and see if your friend can hear you.

How It Works

Your voice makes the can vibrate as you speak into it. The vibrations are carried along the string to the other can which also vibrates, reproducing the sound of your voice so your friend can hear you speaking.

27

Recycling Plastics

Plastic is a very useful material that is cheap and easy to make. This is why we use so much of it. In the USA, two and a half million plastic bottles are used every hour! Most plastic is non-biodegradable which makes it difficult to get rid of. The best way is to recycle it and make something new with it. Oil is used to make many plastics, so recycling also saves oil.

LPs are made from plastic. There are millions of unwanted LPs in the world and they are now being collected and turned into cheque cards!

stuffing for furnishings

bin liners

piping

plant pots

fencing

Wellington boots

squeezy bottles

carrier bags

👁 Eye-Spy

These logos are used on plastic packaging to show that it can be recycled. A different number is used for each type of plastic. Can you find these logos on containers in your home?

A surprising range of objects can be made using recycled plastic, from carrier bags and white squeezy bottles to Wellington boots, plant pots and piping.

Do it yourself

Reuse a plastic bottle to make an unusual plant holder. You may need to ask an adult to help you with the cutting.

1. Find an empty 2 litre plastic drinks bottle and peel off the label. Using a felt tip pen, draw two rings around the bottle, one 8cm from the bottom, the other 13cm from the top as shown on the page opposite.

plastic drinks bottle

scissors

small pot plant

Fast Food

Polystyrene fast food containers trap the heat so that the food does not get cold. They once had to be thrown away, but now they can be recycled.

8cm   13cm

2. Draw two lines, 15mm apart, down the length of the bottle between the two rings. Draw three more sets of lines, evenly spacing them round the bottle. Cut out the large rectangles between your lines.

3. Make two holes in the top of the bottle and thread string through to hang up your container. Finally, put a small pot plant inside.

Plastics for recycling are first sorted into the different types. Then they are washed and shredded into tiny pieces, or chips, before being melted down and turned into something new.

How Can We Help?

- Take plastic bottles and other packaging to your local recycling centre.
- Take a plastic carrier bag with you when you go shopping so you don't need to be given a new one.
- Reuse plastic ice cream tubs as sandwich or freezer boxes.
- Use yoghurt pots for mixing paints or glue.

29

Recycle Your Rags

Old clothes and rags should never be thrown away. Just like glass and paper, rags can be recycled. Some fabrics are ripped up to make a substance called 'shoddy'. This is used to make furniture fabrics, blankets, carpets and even new clothes. Other fabrics are turned into stuffing for mattresses, and some are used as wiping cloths for machinery.

New from Old

This girl is wearing an outfit knitted entirely out of recycled wool.

Some old clothes are collected by charities and are resold or sent to poorer countries. A few clothes are burned as rubbish. But the rest can be recycled.

sent to people in poor countries

recycled as blankets, furnishing fabrics, carpets and clothes

burned as rubbish

Old woollen clothes are used to make shoddy. First they have to be sorted into colours – sometimes as many as 50 different ones!

recycled as stuffing for mattresses

recycled as wiping cloths for factory machinery

Do it yourself

Turn an old sock into a fun puppy puppet. You could even make lots of different animals and put on your own puppet show.

1. Find an old sock and sew up any holes.

2. Using a felt tip pen, draw two ears, two eyes, a nose and a tongue on

floppy ear

pointed ear

tongue

eye

nose

to brightly coloured felt or cotton fabric. Copy the shapes given here, making them as big as you like. Or draw different shapes and make a mouse, a cat, or some other animal.

3. Now glue or sew all the different shapes on to your sock.

4. To use your puppet, put your hand inside the sock so that the heel sits over your knuckles. Push the toe in on itself to form the mouth. Then tap your fingers and thumb together to make your puppet 'talk'.

How Can We Help?

- Take good quality old clothes to jumble sales or charity shops.
- Take damaged old cloths, blankets and materials to a clothes bank. Your local council should be able to tell you where your nearest one is.
- Tear up old towels or sheets and use them as floor cloths or dusters.

Index